Discovering the
Lost World

Written by Caitlin Fraser

Flying Start
to Literacy®

T0342924

Contents

Introduction

We have lived on Earth for hundreds of thousands of years and our urge to explore has left few places untouched. Today, we think we know every corner of our planet. But, do we?

Well, imagine a place where no human has ever lived, a place where only a handful of people have ever set foot. Imagine a place that is so isolated, it has been called "The Lost World".

There is such a place. It is the Foja Mountains in Papua province, New Guinea, which scientists believe was not visited until the scientific expeditions during the last ten years.

Scientists have explored the mountainous area, covered in old-growth rainforest, and discovered new animal species and rare wildlife living there. The Foja Mountains are home to animals that exist nowhere else in the world.

What is old-growth forest?

An old-growth forest has very tall trees that have been growing undisturbed for hundreds of years.

Scientists have discovered new animals in the Foja Mountains.

Pacific Ocean

NORTH AMERICA

The Foja Mountains

AUSTRALIA

Chapter 1

The Lost World

The Foja Mountains have been called "The Lost World" because the area is remote and undisturbed by humans. People live in the foothills of the mountains, which are their traditional lands. But there is no evidence of people ever having lived on the mountains. The mountains' tropical rainforest provides an unspoiled habitat. It is a unique environment for plants and animals.

The mountains rise to over 2000 metres high and are covered by dense forest. The tropical climate means it is warm all year and rains heavily for long stretches of time. Plants grow rapidly all year round, providing shelter and abundant food for the many animals that live in the rainforest. Plants and animals thrive in the pristine rainforest habitat of the Foja Mountains.

The Foja Mountains are covered in rainforest.

Chapter 2

Exploring the Lost World

People have always known about the Foja Mountains. But they were isolated and inaccessible. Scientists and explorers believed that the animals that lived there would remain a secret forever.

> *"It really was like crossing some sort of time warp into a place that people hadn't been to."*
> **–Beehler**

It wasn't until a scientist, Jared Diamond, surveyed the area in a helicopter in 1979 and 1981 that people first saw images of the Foja Mountains. Diamond made observations about a number of birds, but he did not land and collect data or specimens. Dr Bruce Beehler was inspired by Diamond's efforts and he began planning an expedition. Beehler is an ornithologist, which means he is a person who studies birds.

Planning the expedition

Beehler took over 20 years to plan the expedition into the
Foja Mountains. A major obstacle was the difficulty of
reaching the area. The only way to reach the mountain
range was by helicopter, but the thick rainforest canopy
seemed to be unbroken, making it impossible to land. But
Beehler persisted. He flew all over the mountain ranges
looking for a potential landing spot. On his third flight,
he spotted a small clearing in the rainforest, which was
big enough to land a helicopter. This spot flooded each
year and because of this trees, grasses and shrubs did not
grow. It was an ideal place for the helicopter to land.

"It's beautiful, untouched, unpopulated forest; there's no evidence of human impact or presence."
–Beehler

The safety of the members of the expedition in such a remote place was very important. All medical supplies, as well as food stores, had to be taken with them. The scientists also needed to bring the specific tools and equipment required to collect, catch, study and document the wildlife they encountered. They had to carry everything they needed with them.

The small clearing in the rainforest where a helicopter could safely land

Journeys into the unknown

Beehler led two scientific expeditions to the Foja Mountains – in 2005 and 2008. Beehler and a group of scientists flew into the Foja Mountains in a small plane. The scientists were from Australia, Indonesia and the United States. Then a team of scientists and local villagers were transported high into the mountains by helicopter. When they landed, they were in a place where people had never been before. There were no roads and no villages.

Expedition members unload supplies

A view of the campsite high in the Foja Mountains

The scientists lived in tents deep in the forest. They studied and recorded information about the plants and animals living there. Every day, the scientists made fascinating new discoveries. On the first expedition, they found more than 40 new animal species, including new amphibians, reptiles, birds and mammals. The scientists were excited about these new finds, and they all felt sure that many more new species were yet to be discovered.

What is a species?

A species is a scientific classification. All members of a species have features in common, which are unique to them.

"This is one of the last new places to go. This mountain range generates its own species, a little bit like the Galápagos."

–Beehler

The scientists worked day and night to find, study, photograph and write about the new plants and animals they saw. They caught animals in traps and nets, sometimes by hand, in order to study them.

They set up a tent as a laboratory. In this tent, they preserved animal skeletons, skins and collected DNA samples to study in further detail upon their return home. They took photographs, recorded animal sounds and measured, weighed and studied the specimens they found.

A specimen is a sample of something. Scientists collect specimens and study them for similar patterns.

What is DNA?

DNA stands for deoxyribonucleic acid (say *dee-ox-ee-rye-boe-new-clay-ic acid*). It is found inside the cells of living things. DNA has all the information about how that living thing will look and behave.

An ornithologist
records bird calls

The living conditions in the rainforest were difficult for the scientists. They endured torrential rain and flash floods. Rivers could swell by more than two metres in about half an hour. The heavy rain made it difficult to keep things dry and the scientists' clothes and shoes became uncomfortably damp and sodden.

Scientists hiked through heavy mud.

"There was not a single trail, no sign of civilisation, no sign of even local communities ever having been there."

–Beehler

An expedition member
dries out his sodden boots

Scientists had to constantly keep an eye out for
falling branches. They suffered sores from leeches
and painful rashes from stinging plants. Despite
the harsh living conditions, the scientists agreed
that the success of the expeditions made up for
the hardships.

Chapter 3

Amazing discoveries

The scientists made amazing discoveries of new species of animals in the Foja Mountains, including new species of mammals and birds. Discovering new species of animals is important because new discoveries add to what we already know about animals. But finding new species of mammals and birds is rare. Imagine how exciting it was for the scientists to find animals that are not found anywhere else in the world!

The scientists also found species of animals in the mountains that are critically endangered. These important discoveries are vital to preserve these species in the future.

What is a scientific name?

Every living thing is given a scientific name. This name includes the genus (similar to a surname in people) and the species to which it belongs. The name of the genus is written first, followed by the species name. Most scientific names come from the Latin language.

The letters *sp nov* come from the Latin words *species nova* and mean that the species is new and hasn't been given a species name yet.

"Everyone was so transfixed. You are seeing a bird that no Western scientist has ever seen."

–Beehler

Common name
Dwarf wallaby

Scientific name
Dorcopsulus sp nov

Class
Mammal / marsupial

Characteristics
grey fur,
30 centimetres long

Dwarf wallaby

A dwarf wallaby was found and caught by some of the
local village guides who were helping the scientists.
Other dwarf wallabies were seen hopping around in the
forest during the expedition. They are only about 30
centimetres long. The dwarf wallaby is a member of the
kangaroo family and this new species is now the smallest
member of this family.

Common name
Blossom bat

Scientific name
Syconycteris sp nov

Class
Mammal

Characteristics
nocturnal, dark brown fur, large ears, very long tongue

Blossom bat

This new bat species is said to be the "hummingbird of the bat world". It uses its very long tongue to drink nectar out of flowers, similar to a hummingbird or a bee. As it drinks the nectar, it gets pollen on its tongue and, as the bat moves from flower to flower, the pollen is transferred from flower to flower. This pollination enables flowers to begin producing seeds so new plants can grow.

Common name
Long-nosed tree frog

Scientific name
Litoria sp nov

Class
Amphibian

Characteristics
long nose

Long-nosed tree frog

The long-nosed tree frog was found by accident when it was discovered sitting on top of a bag of rice at the campsite. A scientist quickly grabbed the frog. This frog is unique because of its very long nose. When the frog calls out, its nose rises into the air. When the frog is inactive, its nose droops down. The long-nosed tree frog is also known as the Pinocchio tree frog and the spiked-nose tree frog.

Common name
Giant rat (also known as Bosavi woolly rat)

Scientific name
Mallamoys sp nov

Class
Mammal

Characteristics
silver-brown coat

Giant rat

The giant rat was first spotted at night using an infrared camera. The rat showed no fear of humans and often visited the scientists' camp. The giant rat is about 76 centimetres long and weighs up to two kilograms. It is a new species that is about five times the size of a regular rat!

> *"The first time I saw the face of that honeyeater with those wattles was a heart-stopping moment."*
> **–Beehler**

Common name
Wattled smoky honeyeater

Scientific name
Melipotes carolae sp nov

Class
Bird

Characteristics
dark grey, orange wattle

Wattled smoky honeyeater

This new bird species was one of the very first new animals to be discovered by scientists during their expedition. These birds were often seen around the camp. It is called the wattled smoky honeyeater because it has dark grey smoky-coloured feathers and a bright orange wattle (a piece of skin hanging from the neck).

Common name
Bent-toed gecko

Scientific name
Cyrtodactylus
boreoclivus sp nov

Class
Amphibian

Characteristics
25 centimetres
long, webbed feet,
moist skin, bright
yellow eyes

Bent-toed gecko

During a night expedition, the scientists discovered this
new type of gecko. The gecko was spotted when its eye
reflected a scientist's headlamp. A bent-toed gecko's eye
reflection can be seen from about 20 to 30 metres away.
The gecko gets its name from the characteristic curling
of its toes.

Common name
Long-beaked echidna

Scientific name
Zaglossus bruijni

Class
Mammal / monotreme

Characteristics
dark, spiny coat, long snout

Long-beaked echidna

The long-beaked echidna is so rare that only a few people have ever seen one. It is believed that no one has ever seen a baby long-beaked echidna. The scientists were able to pick up the echidna. It had no fear of humans, probably because it had never seen people before. The animal uses its long snout to find worms to eat. Its snout has electroreceptors, which help it to find worms. When it finds a worm, the echidna spears the worm with its barbed tongue.

Common name
Golden-mantled tree kangaroo

Scientific name
Dendrolagus pulcherrimus

Class
Mammal / marsupial

Characteristics
light brown fur, golden stripe on back, pale rings on long tail

Golden-mantled tree kangaroo

The golden-mantled tree kangaroo is critically endangered so the scientists were thrilled to see them on their expedition. Finding this rare tree kangaroo showed that there was no hunting in the area and that animals could live safely. Scientists were able to take the first-ever photo of this animal in the wild. Like all tree kangaroos, the golden-mantled tree kangaroo is arboreal, meaning it spends most of its life in trees.

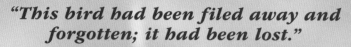

Common name
Berlepsch's six-wired bird of paradise

Scientific name
Parotia berlepschi

Class
Bird

Characteristics
black feathers, bronze patches on chest and head, silver feathers on top of head

Berlepsch's six-wired bird of paradise

This bird of paradise was seen over 100 years ago in another part of the country, but the male of the species hadn't been seen since. On only the second day of the expedition, a male bird of paradise was spotted and the first-ever photographs were taken of it. The bird gets its name from the six silver-tipped wirelike feathers on top of its head.

Chapter 4

The future
of the Lost World

Around the world, habitats are being destroyed and animal species are being wiped out at an alarmingly rapid rate. It is important to protect the unspoilt habitat of the Foja Mountains and the unique animals living there. Further expeditions in the future will likely discover more new animals.

A house in Kwerba village, at the foothills of the mountains

The Foja Mountains are of vital importance to the local people who live at the foothills. The mountains provide fresh water that runs into the rivers. The people rely on the rivers and the rainforest for food. The mountains are also the foundation of their ancient stories and legends.

The Foja Mountains are currently a protected wildlife sanctuary. This preserves the rainforest and keeps the animals living in it safe. There might, however, come a time when there is pressure to log the rainforest and to poach the animals. Most people believe that this should never happen and that the Foja Mountains and the unique animals living there must always be protected.

The rainforest of the Foja Mountains is currently protected. Scientists have explored only a small portion of the rainforest on the Foja Mountains.

Conclusion

The Foja Mountains are one of the few places on Earth that haven't been disturbed by human activity. There is no pollution and animals are not being wiped out or losing their homes. It is a place where animals live safely in their natural habitat.

Scientific expeditions have explored only a very small portion of the rainforest, but the discoveries have been amazing. There are sure to be more expeditions and the discovery of new species in the future. It is exciting to wonder what new secrets might be uncovered in the remote and beautiful habitat of the Foja Mountains. The difficulty will be to allow people to access the area while still preserving its unspoilt, pristine state.

"We just scratched the surface. Anyone who goes there will come back with a mystery."
–Beehler

Index